Women's Work
Is Never Done . . .

Women's Work Is Never Done . . .

Celebrating Everything Women Do

BJ Gallagher

Conari Press

Conari Press
An imprint of Turner Publishing Company
Nashville, Tennessee
www.turnerpublishing.com

Library of Congress Cataloging-in-Publication Data

Hateley, B. J. Gallagher (Barbara J. Gallagher), 1949–
  Women's work is never done : celebrating everything women do / B.J.
Gallagher.
    p. cm.
  ISBN 1-57324-266-7 (alk. paper)
  1. Women. 2. Women—Social conditions. I. Title.
  HQ1155.H38 2006
  305.4--dc22

                              2005027600

Typeset in Truesdell, GillSans, and SignPainter by Jill Feron/FeronDesign
Printed in the United States of America

13 12 11 10 09 08 07 06 8 7 6 5 4 3

For Karen Gallagher,
whose unique blend of skill and charm
makes women's work look easy and elegant.
I'm doubly blessed to count you as both family *and* friend.

All over the world, women's work is essentially cyclical and unending; the tasks are not the kind that lend themselves to closure. And it's not just child-raising. The difference goes back to the organization of hunter-gatherer societies. The men get together and go out for the occasional big kill, a specific event that has a climax, and then it's over.

But the women, who plant and gather, work at continuous tasks that need to be done again and again. This leads them to have more of a process orientation; and when you focus on process rather than achievement or closure, you get more satisfaction from the work itself. You get pleasure from the actual doing of it, rather than from the abstract notion of getting it done.

–DIANA MEEHAN, USC Institute for the Study of Women & Men in Society

CONTENTS

INTRODUCTION

My mother used to shake her head and sigh, "Women's work is never done." As a girl, I didn't know what she meant. Today I know. I've learned that the phrase "working woman" is redundant. All women work—most in their homes, many in the workplace, some in their communities, others in their places of worship—and *all* of us work just to keep body and soul together!

We build and nurture relationships with friends and family. We communicate our desires, demonstrate our feelings, navigate our way through busy days and complex lives. We ovulate, menstruate, gestate, procreate, lactate, meditate, create, animate, illustrate, agitate, aggravate, debate, propagate, litigate, delegate, compensate, radiate, and emulate. Some women even levitate and aviate! Women's work is cyclical, never ending, ever evolving, always important.

This book is a celebration of women who work—and that's all of us!

AFFIRM our own and each other's worth.

Where there is woman there is magic.

—NTOZAKE SHANGE, poet, playwright, performance artist

'ATTA GIRL!

It's so easy for women
to slip into self-doubt
        and feeling inadequate.

After all,
we shoulder a lot of responsibilities—
        being supportive of our mates,
        nurturing our children,
        staying in touch with extended family,
        holding down jobs
        while holding down the fort at home.

No wonder we sometimes feel
        anxious,
                exhausted,
                        insecure,
                                second-guessing ourselves.

We need to know
        we're not alone.

We need to hear
    that other women
        share our experiences.

"Atta girl" never sounded so sweet
        as when coming from the lips
           of another woman.
She understands,
    she's been there, done that.

She gets it—
    she gets *me*.
We take turns
    encouraging,
        supporting,
           cheering one another on.

We learn to do it for ourselves, too.
Just reach right over your shoulder, girl,
    and pat yourself on the back.

You're terrific,
    and you and I both know it.

POSITIVELY GREAT!

Thank goodness for women in the world who "get it." Girlfriends who notice all the things we do well—and comment on them. "What a great outfit—I love the way you combine colors." . . . "Thank you for the thoughtful birthday gift—you're so good at picking out the perfect present." . . . "I love having you as my friend—we always have such a good time together."

I do the same for them. I let other women know when they do something I especially like. I affirm how much I value them as friends—as people. I live by the maxim, "Catch people doing something right," . . . then acknowledge them for it.

No one responds well to guilt and shame. So why is it that people try to scold, nag, nitpick, and fault-find us into changing our ways? Don't they know it doesn't work? Not only is it ineffective, it's infuriating. From the "Stand up straight" of our girlhood to the "You should . . ." we hear every day, I vote we put away the negatives and try to accentuate the positive—for ourselves and others.

Everyone is hungry for appreciation. We all want to be valued, cherished, and respected. Sure, there will always be critics ready to point out our shortcomings. But the women I'm most grateful for are those who celebrate what's *right* with the world—and the people in it!

Tips and Tools for Women @ Work

CATCH PEOPLE DOING SOMETHING RIGHT

The mind is a mismatch detector. It always notices what's wrong before it notices what's right. That's why we are quick to criticize and so slow to compliment. I'll bet most people say ten negative things for every one positive thing they say to others!

Wouldn't you rather be a people praiser than a people critic? For sure, you'd get better results from your relationships—I guarantee it. People want to be around others who make them feel good about themselves.

Ken Blanchard, coauthor of many wonderful business books (including *The One Minute Manager*), taught me to "catch people doing something right"—and I'd like to pass it along to you.

Try an experiment: For the next week, watch the people around you—at work and at home—and when they do something you like, show your approval and appreciation.

(continued)

Here are a few guidelines:

1. Be specific—tell them exactly what they did that you like.
2. Be timely—do it as soon as possible (don't wait three days to show your appreciation).
3. Be sincere—people can tell if you don't really mean it, and it will backfire.
4. Be personal—tell them why you like what they did and how it affects you.

See how people respond to you. See if it makes a difference in how you feel about yourself, too. In fact, you can experiment with "catch *yourself* doing something right" and see what a difference that makes. You might surprise yourself.

BE CURIOUS and ask good questions.

I think, at a child's birth, if a mother could ask a fairy godmother to endow it with the most useful gift, that gift should be curiosity.

—ELEANOR ROOSEVELT, UN delegate, social activist, first lady, wife of President Franklin D. Roosevelt

SCHOOL DAYS

When I came home from school each day
my mother didn't ask me,
    "Did you get the right answer today?"
Instead, she would query,
    "Did you ask a good question today?"

She understood that
asking the right questions
    is much more useful than
    trying to have all the answers.

Asking questions about history
    helps us learn from the past.
Questions regarding biology
    help us understand the natural world
    and our place in it.

Inquiring into anthropology
    helps us learn from others
    who are different from us.
Queries concerning philosophy
    help us determine the meaning of life.

The more I learn,
    the more I realize how valuable
        my mother's lesson is:
Knowing everything isn't the goal;
    being curious about everything is.

How to be CURIOUS . . .

Cultivate a habit of asking good questions.

Understand that we can experience miracles if we're inquisitive.

Realize that we know very little and there's discovery and adventure around every corner.

Inquire into new ideas, people, situations, places.

Open our minds to others' points of view.

Unleash our inner child, who is naturally inquisitive.

Suspend judging and evaluating—there's always time for that later.

Tips and Tools for Women @ Work

INQUIRING MINDS WANT TO KNOW

You can learn a lot by listening. And an important part of listening is asking good questions. You can show others that you care by the quality of questions you pose. You can impress potential employers with the intelligence of your inquiries. You can learn a lot about yourself, too, with thoughtful queries.
   Some samples to choose from:

- How did you get into your line of work?
- What advice would you give someone who wants to have a long, happy marriage?
- If you had your life to live over again, what would you do differently?
- What do you want to be remembered for when you die?
- If you could live anywhere in the world and money was no object, where would you live? Why?

(continued)

- If you won the lottery, what would you do with the money?
- If I wanted some advice on how to be happy, what would you tell me?
- If I could ask you only one question to find out who you really are, what should I ask you?

Ask others. Ask yourself. Ask early. Ask often. There's no such thing as too many questions.

P.S. Be sure to listen to the answers—your own and others'.

The power to question is the basis of all human progress.

—INDIRA GANDHI, prime minister of India

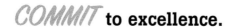 *COMMIT* **to excellence.**

The minute you settle for less than you deserve,

you get even less than you settled for.

—MAUREEN DOWD, syndicated newspaper columnist

EXCELLENCE

Committing to excellence is not the same as committing to perfection. We don't need to become driven, Type A, maniacal perfectionists in order to commit to excellence. Excellence simply means striving for the highest standard that each situation calls for, to the best of your ability.

Few things in life need to be done perfectly; brain surgery is probably one of them—maybe human space shuttle missions, too—and work with hazardous chemicals or radiation. But most everything else does not require the same exacting level of perfection in order to be excellent.

Excellence simply means doing the best job you can with the information and resources you have available, within the time allotted. Being an excellent parent means knowing when to insist that your kids toe the line and when to let things slide. Being excellent at work requires you to work with others, make the most of the time and energy you have, within certain budget constraints. Being excellent in taking care of your body and health means educating yourself about nutrition, eating sensibly, making exercise a regular part of your life, and getting enough rest as well as adequate medical care.

Being excellent does not mean that you have to keep the perfect house, raise the perfect kids, have the perfect body, work at the perfect company in the perfect job. It simply means having the highest standards possible, appropriate to each situation.

Sometimes, if something is worth doing, it may be worth doing only modestly well . . . if other, more important things require a higher level of performance. Only *you* can decide which thing you need or want to do perfectly and which things you can simply do well.

We are what we repeatedly do.

Excellence, then, is not an act, but a habit.

—ARISTOTLE, ancient Greek philosopher

How to achieve EXCELLENCE . . .

Eagerly pursue your goals in life.

Xpand your skills, knowledge, and experience.

Commit to integrity and keeping your word.

Express yourself clearly, succinctly, appropriately.

Listen to your conscience.

Learn from others you admire and respect.

Embrace the challenges that life presents you.

Never waste time and energy "spinning your wheels"
   on things you can't control or influence.

Compromise when it's appropriate.

Enroll others in helping you be your best.

Tips and Tools for Women @ Work

MAKE YOUR COMMITMENT TO EXCELLENCE

Decide what project or aspect of your life you want to commit to being excellent. Start with just one. Don't try to take on every aspect of your life all at once.

- Write it down.
- Decide how to measure your excellence. How will you know when you're successful? If you don't have a way of measuring it, you'll have a hard time achieving it.
- Read it out loud and see how you feel when you read it.
- Read it to a trusted friend, someone who will encourage and support you in your quest for excellence.
- Enroll others, a support team, to help you stay the course.
- Periodically check your progress and see how you're doing.
- Celebrate progress along the way, no matter how small.
- When you feel you've achieved excellence in your chosen area or project, or you're at least well on your way, then pick a second excellence target area for yourself and start the process all over again.

You know what real power is? Real power is when you are doing exactly what you are supposed to be doing the best it can be done. Authentic power. There's a surge, there's a kind of energy field that says, "I'm in my groove." And nobody has to tell you, "You go, girl," because, you know, you're already gone.

—OPRAH WINFREY, actress, talk show host, media executive

DIG deeply into life's mysteries.

Chance is perhaps the pseudonym of
God when He did not want to sign.
–ANATOLE FRANCE, Nobel Prize-winning author

Every situation—nay, every moment—is of infinite worth;
for it is the representative of a whole eternity.
–JOHANN WOLFGANG VON GOETHE, German poet

THE MYSTERY OF BEING IN THE FLOW

Creativity is a mystery to me. I don't understand exactly what it is or how it works. It seems to be some sort of energy, like electricity, that I can't see but I can feel it and see its effects. Being in the flow of creativity is a mystical experience . . . feeling in sync with life forces and the universe. One of the loveliest experiences I had with the mystery of flow occurred recently when I took a class on furniture painting.

We were instructed to bring a small piece of old furniture for our class project. I brought a yard sale coffee table. Our instructor gave us the basics, and we began painting—first the base colors, then the decorative designs on top.

And as I worked, I remembered another class I'd taken, called "The Artist's Way." What I remembered was, "You have to give yourself permission to make *bad* art before you can make good art."

"Bad art?" I said to myself. "I can do that." So I gave myself permission to use my coffee table as a trial-and-error piece, a sampler, an experiment, an opportunity to explore this new art form.

We painted all day, taking a break for lunch. At the end of the class, my table was not done, so I bought some more paint from the shop where the class was held, and took my project home to finish.

I had a bite of dinner and resumed painting. I was on a roll. I was having so much fun—painting flowers, squiggles, words, phrases, dots, symbols, textures, and colors all over the table—even the underside. I decided not to go to bed until it was done. I wanted to stay in the flow.

The hours rolled by, and I kept painting . . . . lost in my fun and lost in time. Finally, it was finished. I was happy. I went to the kitchen and glanced at a clock—it was 3 a.m.! I was shocked. Never in my life have I gotten so immersed in anything that I lost track of time. What an amazing experience! It was as if time fell away while I was in the flow of painting. You've heard of out-of-body experiences? Well, this was an out-of-time experience.

I came away from it with a new appreciation for the mystery of the creative process—and for what it's like to be in the flow. I loved it. I felt completely happy, at peace, free from any worldly cares and concerns. Any stress I had disappeared. . . .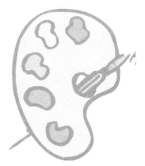

And I had a new coffee table.

WOMEN'S MYSTERIES

To be a woman is to be a mystery,
        and as many readers will attest,
nothing beats a good mystery!

So dig deep, sister sleuth. . . .
Look far and wide,
        and don't forget to look inside.

You certainly can't judge a book
        by its cover,
                or a woman either.

Enjoy your inquiry;
        explore what intrigues you;
        inquire into what puzzles you;
        seek answers to vexing questions.
Women wonder,
        and
women are a wonder!
We are wonder-full.

Tips and Tools for Women @ Work

DIGGING DEEP

There are, of course, many possible paths to exploring our mysteries—science, psychology, medicine, meditation, travel, philosophy, theology, journaling, and more.

Start with a question you'd like answered . . . . the kind of question it is will suggest ways to explore its mystery.

- If your question is something about how your body works, you might read anatomy books or take a class in human physiology.
- If you're curious about the universe, you might buy yourself a microscope or telescope.
- If the meaning of life is the mystery you'd like to explore, reading theology, going to spiritual lectures, studying great philosophers could all be avenues of exploration.

(continued)

- If outer space intrigues you, a visit to a planetarium or observatory could begin to quench your thirst for understanding.
- If it's inner space that mystifies you, perhaps some time in psychotherapy would be part of your journey, as well as reading the works of Jung, Freud, Rogers, Maslow, and others.

Consider taking a trip to an exotic location . . . . take up meditation . . . . keep a journal . . . . talk with experts or gurus about the mystery that captivates you. Follow your mystery wherever it takes you.

Exuberance is beauty.

—WILLIAM BLAKE, English painter, engraver, poet

EXPRESS **ourselves authentically.**

About all you can do in life is be who you are.
Some people will love you for you. Most will love you for
what you can do for them, and some won't like you at all.

--RITA MAE BROWN, feminist, author, educator

Always be a first-rate version of yourself,
instead of a second-rate version of somebody else.

--JUDY GARLAND, actress, singer,
petite performer with a huge stage presence

HONESTLY!

Very young children are totally authentic. They express their delight and displeasure with equal intensity—pulling no punches, hedging no bets. They just let it all hang out, unconcerned for what others may think. You always know where you stand with a toddlers—their wishes and moods clear and unambiguous.

But socialization soon teaches youngsters to put on masks, disguising their true feelings. Adults teach them to put on a happy face because no one wants to be around a grumpypants. We teach children to squelch their requests because it's rude to ask for presents. And we routinely toss verbal wet blankets on them because their noisy exuberance is a bit much to take sometimes.

It's all done with the best of intentions, of course. We want our little ones to develop social skills to fit into the adult world. But in the process, we impart a subtle, not-so-positive message: "It's not OK to express your feelings. It makes others uncomfortable. They might not like you—they might even punish you." And so they develop layer upon layer of filters, screens, censors, and masks—all designed to keep them safe and to maintain social order.

Fast forward to adulthood, and we wonder why we feel lonely, even in our own families sometimes. We long for emotional connection, but we can't reach each other through the layers of masks.

Expressing ourselves authentically means removing some of our masks, shedding some of our layers of social niceties, much as we would slip out of sweaters that are too stifling. It's a slow, gradual process of trial and error, learning what works as we go. It doesn't mean that we become toddlers again—blurting out indiscriminately. No, authentic expression means being true to yourself without bruising or bullying others.

Expressing ourselves authentically involves being clear and honest while at the same time accurately gauging the listening of others. Knowing your audience as well as knowing yourself.

Be clear about your motives when you speak. For honesty without love is simply brutality—but love without honesty is just sentimentality. Expressing ourselves authentically means speaking our truth with love.

WHAT DOES IT MEAN TO BE AUTHENTIC?

Aware

Understand:

Tactful

Honest

Empathetic

Natural

Tuned in

Intimate

Caring

Tips and Tools for Women @ Work

SPEAKING AUTHENTICALLY

What gets in the way of our speaking authentically? It's usually fear—fear that someone might not like us, fear of hurting another's feelings, fear of being different from others, fear of retaliation, fear of rocking the boat. Many of us were raised to please others—authority figures in particular, as well as friends and family. So we keep quiet, bite our tongues, and carry around all sorts of feelings and thoughts that we fear are too dangerous to express.

But there's a price we pay for our silence. In silencing our voices, we risk turning ourselves into pressure cookers of pent-up emotions—with the potential to blow up in destructive rages or tantrums. Or we act out passive-aggressively, finding subtle ways to express the inexpressible. Many of us use food, alcohol, drugs, shopping, or some other substance or activity to stuff down our "unacceptable" emotions and ideas.

(continued)

How do we learn to speak up and speak out without our worlds coming apart? How can we muster the courage to express our true feelings and thoughts?

Start small. Take baby steps in your journey to fuller self-expression. Some women use qualifiers to help themselves feel safe in expressing opinions with which others might not agree. "It's just my opinion . . . ," "It seems to me that . . . ," "From my perspective it seems like . . . ," and other such phrases can help you test the waters around you and take some tentative steps toward expressing yourself more authentically.

Gradually you want to drop the use of qualifiers and speak without them. I find it helpful if I think of it as speaking *my* truth, not *the* truth. Using comments like, "I feel . . . ," "I think . . . ," "I really love it when . . . ," "No, that won't work for me . . . ," "I'm just not comfortable with that . . . ," and similar phrases. The idea is to use "I language" not "you language." I speak up about what I feel, think, don't want, feel uncomfortable with, and what won't work for me. Then I pause and see what others say or do.

You may have to take a deep breath in doing this. You may have to repeat a mantra in your mind: "I won't die if people disagree with me," or "I won't die if others don't like me." But you might be pleasantly surprised, and find that others like you more when you are more authentic in how you deal with them. Try it and see!

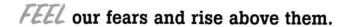 **FEEL** **our fears and rise above them.**

When I'm about to take a risk,
I consider the down side. If it's not death, I do it.
–NANCY SARDELLA, President/CEO,
Women's Referral Service & Women's Yellow Pages

FEAR CAN BE A PLUS

When I left my corporate job to start my own business as a writer and speaker, a good friend told me, "Fear is a great motivator." We both laughed. He was talking about financial fear, of course. When you're a single mom and decide to become self-employed, you suddenly realize that your future really *is* in your own hands, and whether you succeed or fail is totally up to you. It's exhilarating . . . and terrifying.

Fear motivates me to keep new projects in the pipeline at all times. Fear helps me meet deadlines. Fear enables me to focus on my priorities and not get distracted by too many things that are fun, but not income producing.

On a personal level, fear reminds me to lock my doors and turn on the alarm in my home when I leave. Fear tells me to look both ways before I drive through an intersection. Fear is especially vigilant in nudging me to watch in the rearview mirror for those black and white cars with the red lights on top.

Fear tells me to get my regular mammograms and checkups. Fear reminds me to take my vitamins. Fear gets me out of the house every morning for a two- or three-mile hike with my dog. Fear of illness and infirmity makes me want to take care of my body.

Fear takes the form of butterflies in my stomach before I deliver a keynote speech or teach a seminar. I channel that fear in a positive way—it makes me alert, on point, lively, and dynamic. That kind of fear is fuel for my performance, helping me shine and sparkle.

I think my friend's point was that fear isn't always a bad thing—some fears are healthy and helpful. They keep us on track and in focus. We can use our anxiety, tension, and fear in positive ways—to give us energy, motivation, and determination to get our work done, to compete and excel, and to perform at the top of our game.

I have to admit . . . sometimes fear is my friend.

WHAT IS FEAR?

False

Evidence

Appearing

Real

Tips and Tools for Women @ Work

INSPIRATION

Sometimes a book title is so great that you don't even have to read the book to get its message—you just hold onto the title. Not that I'm saying you should stop reading books ... oh, no! By all means, read the books! But sometimes a title says it all—it's like a golden nugget of wisdom I can carry with me.

Here are a few of my favorites:

- *Feel the Fear and Do It Anyway*
- *What Would You Do If You Had No Fear?*
- *Fearless Living: Live without Excuses and without Regret*

Think of some favorite book titles or inspirational quotes that have helped you in the past. Write them down on sticky notes and post them where you can see them.

Keep a small notebook or a pad of sticky notes with you so you can write them down when you find them. Look in the bookstore or the library. Look at marquees in front of churches. Listen to people you admire and write down words of wisdom they say. Use nuggets of inspiration to give you courage and encouragement when you need it.

> Courage is being scared to death
> but saddling up anyway.
>
> —JOHN WAYNE, movie actor and Western icon

***GIVE* 110 percent to life each day.**

One plus one is two.

Two plus two is four.

But five will get you ten

if you know how to work it.

—MAE WEST, witty, sexy silver screen actress

110 PERCENT

Flat out . . .
    Full bore . . .
        Pedal to the metal . . .
        Full tilt . . .
That's how I choose to live.
You ask me, "Why?"
I reply, "Why not?"

Life is like a fabulous buffet
    spread out before me.
I want to help myself
    to as much as my plate can possibly hold.
I love to savor
    the sights and sounds,
        the smells and tastes,
           the sensation of experiences
each and every day.

Some will be sweet,
        others might be bitter,
but it's all fine—
        part and parcel
            of life.

When in doubt,
say "Yes."
Take a chance,
        go for the gusto,
            carpe diem,
you know what I mean.

My challenge is to
        plan like I'll live forever,
and live as if each day
        is my last.

Tips and Tools for Women @ Work

LIVING A RICH, FULL LIFE

What does it mean to give 110 percent to life each day? Living at a frenetic pace? No. Becoming a hyper maniac? No again.

To give 110 percent is to make the most of what life presents us with. Sometimes it even means doing less but savoring it more.

One of the best tools I can offer is the following question:

What's the best use of my time right now?

Ask yourself this question frequently throughout the day. Sometimes the answer will surprise you. Perhaps the answer will be "Take a nap." Another time it might be "Stop my housework and play with my kids." Maybe the answer will be "Balance the checkbook" or "Work on my taxes." Or maybe "Mow the lawn."

Your answer to the question, "What's the best use of my time right now?" will vary from moment to moment, hour to hour, as you go through your day. But it's not the specific answer that is so important—it's asking the question.

This question will keep you in the moment—fully aware of how precious your time is and accountable to yourself for how you live your life. Asking the question helps keep you from running on "automatic pilot" and missing your life.

HEED **our own intuitive wisdom.**

It is only by following your deepest instinct that you can
lead a rich life, and if you let your fear of consequence
prevent you from following your deepest instinct,
then your life will be safe, expedient and thin.

—KATHARINE BUTLER Hathaway, American writer

Blue Hawaii

Jeff and I were scheduled to go to Hawaii in early summer to conduct a workshop at a professional conference. We had known each other for years, since we were both management consultants, but had never had the opportunity to work together before. Jeff had called me months earlier, asking if I was interested in getting on the program for this conference. My mouth said "Yes" but something in my body said "No."

As the months rolled by, that "No" feeling got stronger. I kept trying to ignore it, since I'd made a commitment to Jeff and our proposal had been accepted by the conference organizers. But the feeling just wouldn't go away.

Finally, the "No" I was feeling became so insistent that I had to pay attention. I called Jeff.

"Jeff, this is gonna sound totally crazy, but I can't go to the conference next month. I don't even have a logical reason why . . . all I know is that my intuition is telling me not to go. The feeling gets stronger the closer we get to the conference—it's like every cell in my body is screaming, 'Don't go! You're not supposed to be there.' So I feel badly for letting you down—but I just have to heed that intuition. I don't know what it's about—all I know is I can't go."

"I completely understand," Jeff replied (and he's the kind of spiritual guy who really does understand). "Of course you must go with your intuition."

"Can you get someone else to do the workshop with you?" I asked.

"No," he replied. "Don't worry about it. I'll just do it myself."

"Thank you so much for understanding," I said. "I feel a little embarrassed, not having any logical reason. But I've learned to heed my intuition . . . and whenever I let my head overrule my intuition, I always regret it."

"You're absolutely right," he agreed. "So don't worry about me or the workshop."

"Thanks, Jeff." And I hung up.

The next few weeks rolled by, and I went about my normal work and forgot the conference in Hawaii. Then one day I got an urgent call from my mother, telling me my stepfather had had a heart attack and was in the hospital. I jumped in my car and drove to San Diego to be with her. I met her at the hospital and we spent the afternoon waiting for the doctors to give us some news on his condition.

At one point, I was standing by the nurses' station talking to the nurse on duty. I glanced at the calendar on the wall behind her. Suddenly I realized this was the day I had been scheduled to be conducting that workshop in Hawaii!

I smiled. So *this* was what my intuition had been telling me: I was supposed to be here helping my family, not in Hawaii.

A week later, when Jeff returned from the conference, I told him the story. It confirmed what we both already believed—that intuition is a unique sort of wisdom that needs to be respected and heeded.

WHAT IS INTUITION?

Internal

Natural

True

Unmistakable

Instinctive

Tuned in

Insightful

On the mark

Never fails

Tips and Tools for Women @ Work

How Does Your Intuition Speak to You?

Do all women experience intuition in the same way? How can you tell the difference between your intuition and other feelings, like fear or insecurity, like longing and desire? When is it intuition and when is it rationalization?

- Recall an instance when you were confident of your intuition. What did you feel in your body?
- Recall an instance when you were uncertain of your intuition. How did you decide whether to heed it or not?
- Is your intuition always right, or has it led you astray?
- How do you describe or explain your intuition to others?

 **new projects and possibilities.**

The moment one definitely commits oneself, then
Providence moves, too. All sorts of things occur to help
one that would never have otherwise occurred.

–JOHANN WOLFGANG VON GOETHE, German poet

BEGINNINGS

I love new beginnings. I relish the excitement and anticipation, infused with a touch of fear. . . .

- ✳ Sitting down to a blank piece of paper—with pure potential in front of me
- ✳ Moving into a new home or office—with the challenge of arranging furniture, supplies, objects, and art to suit my taste and lifestyle
- ✳ Beginning a new love affair—with dreams of "happily ever after" dancing in my imagination

Starting a new project of any kind lifts my spirits, stimulates my creativity, and refreshes me with new energy, limitless possibilities.

Oh, I *love* new beginnings!

WHAT LIES AHEAD . . . ? POSSIBILITIES

Pure potential

Opening up

Surprising

Satisfying

Inventiveness

Beginnings

Intuitiveness

Leaping in

Inquisitiveness

Testing your limits

Impulsiveness

Eager

Successes

Tips and Tools for Women @ Work
NEW BEGINNINGS SOMETIMES REQUIRE ENDINGS FIRST

We bring about new beginnings by deciding to bring
about endings. To renew your life you must be
willing to change, to make an effort to leave behind the
things that compromise your wholeness.
The universe rushes to support you whenever
you attempt to take a step forward.
—SUSAN L. TAYLOR, former editor of *Essence* magazine,
considered the inspirational grandmother of black publishing

In order to begin something new, often we have to let go of
something else. If our lives are completely full, there is no room
for anything or anyone new to come in. It is impossible to start
something new if nothing old ever ends.

Here are some questions to ask yourself:

- In what areas of my life would I like something or someone new?
- What would I be willing to give up to create space for something new?
- Is the price of letting go too high? Too scary? Too painful?
- Is the fear of change holding me back?
- What do I have to lose by ending something that is no longer satisfying or meaningful to me?
- What do I have to gain?

The great thing in this world is not so much where
we are, but in what direction we are moving.

—OLIVER WENDELL HOLMES, American author and physician

JUGGLE many roles and duties . . .
while making it look easy!

Women are having to do way too much.

They are multitasking, working long hours, and they are

still responsible for most of what happens with the family;

they are caregivers, best friends, listeners;

they are amazing, amazing people.

–Dawn Tarnofsky-Ostroff, Lifetime television executive

MULTI-TASKING

Multi-tasking doesn't do justice
to what women really do . . .
        miracle working is more like it!

We keep the home fires burning
        while putting out fires at work.
We make to-do lists,
        grocery lists,
                and lists of assets and liabilities.
We wear our power suits,
        go power walking,
                eat Power Bars,
                        and power through our weekend chores.

We hold together our families,
        put together a cute outfit,
                pull together at work,
                        and glue together broken toys.

We juggle our time,
      projects,
         and
         commitments,
balance work and family
      as well as checkbooks.

And we do it all
      while looking our best.
My mother told me that
      "women's work is never done."
Now I know why!

LIVING IN THE TENSION

When I first started working full time, my son Michael was eleven. I had spent the previous seven years in school full time, while single-handedly raising my son. I was accustomed to spending most of time at home studying; Michael was used to coming home from school to mom and a snack.

Now suddenly, I was gone all day every day, and Michael became a latchkey kid. It was hard on both of us.

One day I complained to my boss, "I feel torn. When I'm doing a great job at work, my kid gets lonely and starts acting out. Then I start spending more time with him and I feel like my work suffers. No matter which way I move, it seems I'm not doing justice to one or the other—my family or my work."

"Join the club," my boss replied. "Welcome to the world of working parents. I can guarantee you—all working mothers feel the same push/pull that you're experiencing . . . and I'll bet a lot of fathers do, too."

"What do you do about it?" I asked her, hoping for a magic solution.

"Deal with it," she replied. "There *is* no easy answer. Just learn to live in the tension between work and family, and do the best you can."

Somehow her answer *did* make me feel better. At least I knew I wasn't alone.

Tips and Tools for Women @ Work

THE DIALECTICAL NATURE OF REALITY

Juggling role, projects, activities, and priorities is not an either/or proposition—it's a both/and proposition. We don't choose either work *or* family; we choose work *and* family. We live in the tension between competing demands, desires, and dreams. The notion of achieving "balance" on any permanent basis is useless.

Life is lived in the dialectical tension of polar opposites—pulling one way, then the other. Consider the opposites listed here. Where do you find yourself on the continuum between each?

WORK . . . . FAMILY
INDIVIDUALITY . . . . CONFORMITY
GIVING . . . . RECEIVING
MALE . . . . FEMALE
YOUNG . . . . OLD
PRIVATE . . . . PUBLIC
STABILITY . . . . CHANGE

Get used to the tension. It's normal. *You're* normal.

You need not feel guilty about not being able to keep
your life perfectly balanced. Juggling everything is too difficult.
All you really need to do is catch it before it hits the floor!

–CAROL BARTZ, CEO, Autodesk, Inc.

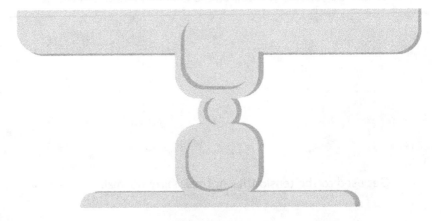

KEEP our sense of humor, especially when others have lost theirs.

If evolution was worth its salt, by now it should've evolved

something better than survival of the fittest. . . .

I think a better idea would be survival of the wittiest.

—JANE WAGNER, playwright, author

LAUGHTER IS GOOD MEDICINE

Like most kids, my son got his share of scrapes and bruises, and sometimes more serious wounds. I recall one trip to the emergency room when he was five: he had tried to climb through a barbed wire fence and cut his face about half an inch below his eye. It was bleeding profusely and I was terrified.

When we arrived at the ER, we were promptly ushered into a curtained exam area. A few minutes later the ER doctor came through the curtain and introduced herself. As she bent over to examine my son's facial wound, she almost hit her head on the adjustable light that hung over the exam table. Looking up, she pushed it out of the way saying, "Oops, I almost hit my head! I better be careful or I'll need a doctor!" She smiled at my son, and he and I both relaxed.

I marveled at her effective use of humor to defuse a very tense situation. Her humor was self-deprecating and funny. It worked like a charm. She'll never know it, but she taught me a helpful skill that day. Appropriate humor can help you and others deal with all kinds of tough situations. For surely, if you don't laugh, you'll cry.

THE GIFT OF LAUGHTER . . .

Loving life, with its ups and downs

Appreciating what's right with the world

Understanding your own quirks and eccentricities

Going for the guffaw along with the gusto

Having fun wherever and whenever you can

Taking yourself lightly (while taking life seriously)

Eager to embrace life's lunacies

Ready to giggle at every opportunity

Tips and Tools for Women @ Work

REMEMBER: NO ONE WILL DIE FROM THIS

Remember your sense of humor—mixed-up,
badly organized plans are not life-threatening—and
you can still have fun while everyone
else is running around in chaos.
—RICHARD FEYNMAN'S (physicist, teacher,
raconteur, musician)advice to his daughter, Michelle

Being able to keep your sense of humor when everything is going awry is not something you're necessarily born with—it's a skill you can develop. It requires learning to reframe situations: to take a mistake and see something funny in it; to view a problem as a puzzle to be solved rather than a source of misery; to see confusion as an opportunity to be creative in sorting it out; to take mishaps in stride, even finding humor in your predicament.

- Think of someone you know who has a great sense of humor. How does he or she handle the "bad" things in life? Watch and listen to that person and see if you can learn from him or her. Pay attention to how he or she finds the humorous in even the most difficult situations.
- Think of some current problem you're facing—can you find anything amusing about it? Can you use your sense of humor to alleviate some of your stress from the problem?
- Are there bad things that have happened in your past that today you laugh about? What does that tell you about your sense of humor?

Laughter is the closest distance between two people.

—Victor Borge, Danish musician, comedian

LISTEN with love.

When someone you love has difficulties, listen.
When you're feeling terrible that you can't
provide a cure, listen. When you don't know what
to offer the people you care about,
listen, listen, listen.
--BERNIE SIEGEL, physician and author

HEART SOUNDS

Someone wise once told me,
"The greatest gift
    you can give someone
        is the gift of the interested listener."

But no one had to tell you that . . .
    you already knew.

Dearest friend, you listen not just with your ears,
but with your heart,
    your mind,
        your soul,
            your entire being.

You listen between the lines
paying attention
to what I don't say,
    as well as what I do.

You genuinely want to know
    what's going on with me.

You listen
    to the language
        of my heart.

With the gift of listening, comes the gift of healing.

—CATHERINE DE HUECK DOHERTY, Catholic author

THE GIFT OF LISTENING

Listening is a gift we give to *others*:

- ❋ Listening tells the other person that they're important.
- ❋ Listening shows others that we genuinely care.
- ❋ Listening says, "I value you, your thoughts, ideas, and feelings."
- ❋ Listening is love.

Listening is a gift we give *ourselves* as well:

- ❋ Listening gives us the opportunity to grow wise by learning from others' experience.
- ❋ Listening gives us a chance to see the world through others' eyes and perhaps discover something new.
- ❋ Listening enables us to feel another person's pain and sadness, as well as their joy and delight. We get connected to others through our shared feelings.
- ❋ Listening provides us with the opportunity to hear God speaking to us through others.

Tips and Tools for Women @ Work

LEARNING TO REALLY LISTEN

We all think we're good listeners, but in reality, most of us aren't. We're too busy reacting to what the other person is saying and planning our response.

What can we do to become better listeners? Try this:

- Maintain eye contact. Steady eye contact tells the other person that you're paying attention, you're honest, you're not intimidated.
- Resist the urge to say, "Oh, I had something like that happen to me, too," and then launch into your own story. This is a common mistake many people make. You're not building rapport by sharing a similar experience—what you're really doing is taking center stage yourself.
- Instead of sharing a similar story, just keep your attention on the speaker. Let them know you're still with listening:

  "Oh, that must have been so hard for you."
  "Thanks for sharing that with me; that's amazing."
  "Oh my, what a thing to have happen . . ."

The point is, keep listening, keep your attention on the other person.

There are people who,
instead of listening to what is being said to them,
are already listening to what they are going to say themselves.

—ALBERT GUINON, British actor

MANAGE our time effectively.

Most people are so busy knocking themselves out
trying to do everything they think they should do,
they never get around to do what they want to do.

—KATHLEEN WINDSOR, author of the bawdy novel *Forever Amber.*

ON TIME, ON TRACK

"Time's a'wastin',"
    Mom would warn
       in her brisk, efficient way.
Always bustling
    and brimming with energy,
she didn't believe
    in wasting time,
       or anything else,
          for that matter.
To-do lists and calendars,
    timelines and timetables,
       clocks and timers—
we had plenty of tools
    to keep track of things.
For households are
like train stations,
    with comings and goings
       and some just passing through.
Men may drive the trains,
    but we women
       make sure they're on time.

GETTING STARTED

Like many people, I have a problem with procrastination, especially when it comes to starting a new project. I futz around with this and that—doing laundry, cleaning the cat box, running errands, sorting out a closet—all the while feeling the tension and anxiety build in my shoulders and neck. Sometimes the tension is so bad, I get a headache. But still I delay sitting down and beginning what I have to do. Why is it so hard to get started?

I was complaining to my good friend Jaime about my problem. He listened sympathetically and then asked me, "Have you ever seen a chicken lay an egg?"

"No," I replied, "I haven't."

"Well, for a while the chicken just walks around the yard kind of fussing and fretting," Jaime explained. "She pecks at the ground, preens her feathers, clucks a bit, and acts edgy and irritable. Finally, after considerable time spent doing all this fussing, she sits down and lays the egg."

"Hey, that's me!" I exclaimed.

"Perhaps all those distractions that you get into before you start a project—perhaps all that is simply part of your creative process," Jaime said. "Maybe you're not procrastinating at all—you're just giving your mind, body, and spirit time to get aligned in order to begin working."

"I like that," I replied. "It makes sense to me. Maybe I just need to factor that into my time management and allow myself the time to futz around before I sit down to lay my 'golden egg.'"

Jaime's metaphor has helped me a lot. I no longer beat myself up for "wasting time" when I have work to get done, especially writing. I see that my pre-writing time as some sort of psychic space and time in which I am mustering the energy, gathering my thoughts, and getting ready to launch into the adventure of a new project.

Only one little problem . . . I seem to be eating a lot of sunflower seeds lately!

If we take care of the moments, the years will take of themselves.

—MARIA EDGEWORTH, British author

Tips and Tools for Women @ Work

MANAGING YOUR LIFE-TIME

Today's woman has ten things she needs to do, but time enough to do only six.

Her challenge is to pick the most important six to do .... then go to sleep at night not worrying about the four she had to let go.

Make a list of the top five values you hold most dear. You can choose among travel, family, spiritual life, health, career, money, friends, golf, biking, gardening, pets, art, music, reading—or any other activity, person(s), or arena of life that is most important to you.

Once you have your top five, rank order them—from #1 being most important to #5 being least.

Now, make copies of these top five life priorities. Write them on sticky notes and put them in places where you'll see them daily . . . your bathroom mirror, your computer monitor, the fridge, the dashboard of your car, your calendar, and so on.

(continued)

As you go through each day and have to choose how to spend your time, refer to your top five list. Ask yourself, "Does what I'm doing right now support what I value?" When you have to choose between doing X or doing Y, ask yourself, "Which one is aligned with my top five values?"

Having these little sticky note reminders of your top five priorities around you will help you make smart choices with your time and energy. Think of them as sticky little yardsticks to help you stick to what you value.

Time is the coin of your life. It is the only coin you have,

and only you can determine how it will be spent.

Be careful lest you let other people spend it for you.

—CARL SANDBURG, American poet

NURTURE **relationships
at work and at home.**

★

One's life has value so long as one attributes
value to the life of others, by means of love,
friendship, indignation, and compassion.
—SIMONE DE BEAUVOIR, French existentialist and author

THE BEST RELATIONSHIPS ARE . . .

Reciprocal

Ebbing and flowing over time

Long lasting

Authentic

Trusting

Interdependent

Open minded

Not threatened by differences or conflict

Supportive

Humorous

Interesting

Personally fulfilling

Satisfying

INTERDEPENDENCE

The older I get, the more I understand and appreciate my relationships. It is the people in my life who provide support, encouragement, and help when I need it, as well as ideas, feedback, and suggestions when I ask.

As a child, I remember that I could play for hours with neighborhood kids I liked. I sacrificed perfect grades to spend more time with fun classmates.

When I entered the world of work, I discovered that business is all about relationships—with coworkers, bosses, clients, customers, vendors, and others. Work is not a mysterious science of finance, strategy, or marketing—it's about *people* connecting to other people.

Our brains are wired for relationships. We are highly social creatures. We live longer, stay healthier, achieve more success, and feel happier when we have a strong network of personal and professional relationships.

Women have always known this. We instinctively tend and befriend. We listen, empathize, advise, help, give, and support others in every possible way. We provide the social glue that keeps families and communities together. We understand that independence is good, but only when balanced with healthy interdependence.

Tips and Tools for Women @ Work

GIVE AND TAKE

Relating to others is an organic process, it seems to me. Relationships have a beginning, a middle, and an end. They ebb and flow like the tides.

They have seasons ... a springlike blossoming, a summer of relaxed enjoyment, a fall of cooling change, and a winter of dormancy ... then the cycle starts all over again.

The best relationships are balanced, reciprocal, as we exchange attention, love, time, support, listening, energy, and sometimes much more. Think about the best relationship you have with another person—it could be your best friend, your spouse, your son or daughter, a neighbor, your mom or aunt, or another family member.

Make a balance sheet of your relationship with that person, listing all the things that you gladly give him or her, as well as all the things that he or she gives to you.

- Is your list of "gives" and "gets" fairly evenly balanced?
- Has it changed over time? Would your list have looked very different a couple of years ago?
- Has that relationship ever felt out of balance to you? If so, what did you do to bring it into balance, or did it just adjust itself over time?
- Can you think of anything else you'd like to give to that person that you're not currently giving? Anything new you'd like to get in return?
- What can you learn about successful relationships from the one you used for this exercise? Anything you can carry into other relationships in your life?

You cannot hope to build a better world without improving individuals. To that end, each of us must work for our own improvement and, at the same time, share a general responsibility for all humanity, our particular duty being to aid those to whom we think we can be most useful.

—MADAME MARIE CURIE, Nobel Prize-winning physicist who discovered radium, paving the way for nuclear physics and cancer therapy

OWN our own lives.

I walked for miles at night along the beach, composing
bad blank verse and searching for someone wonderful
who would step out of the darkness and change my life.
It never crossed my mind that that person could be me.
—ANNA QUINDLEN, Pulitzer Prize-winning journalist and author

CLAIMING MY LIFE

There wasn't just one moment when I claimed ownership of my life . . . there have been several, maybe even many. The first one I recall was when I was twenty-one years old, the mother of a two-and-a-half-year-old, and unhappily married. I had no college education; my job experience consisted of waitressing and working as a secretary in offices; and I was living in a city where I knew few people, having moved there a year earlier because of my husband's job. My parents were living on the other side of the country—it might as well have been on the other side of the world as far as I was concerned, for how could they help me from so far away?

After much anguished soul searching, I decided to leave my husband and take my toddler son with me. I had no idea where I would go or what I would do, but what I did know gave me the confidence to make the break—I knew I was young, smart, healthy, and resourceful, and I would figure something out!

In that moment, I found freedom.

My second moment of freedom came a year later. I had moved back east to live with my parents while I tried to sort out my life and get going in a new direction. But somehow, the Cinderella myth of my girlhood was still with me. I kept waiting for a new man to show up to save me from my predicament.

My estranged husband kept trying to win me back, but somehow I knew it would never work. I dated other men, a couple of whom seemed promising, but it didn't work out. And I knew that I couldn't live at home forever—my dad and mom were very generous, but I knew that staying with them wasn't the answer either.

Then the epiphany: It dawned on me that there *was* no handsome prince riding to my rescue. My husband couldn't save me; other men weren't going to save me; and my dad couldn't save me either. Whatever life I was going to have, I was going to have to make it myself. I had to go out and build my own life—create my own future. I was scared but excited at the same time. That's how those moments of empowerment are—thrilling and terrifying all at once.

Today I can truly say that I own my own life. I own it all—the good, the bad, and the ugly. It's all mine. And I embrace it with love and joy. It's wonderful to be my own woman!

You need to claim the events of your life to make yourself yours.
—ANNE WILSON SCHAEF, author of *Meditations for Women Who Do Too Much*

Tips and Tools for Women @ Work

REFRAINING FROM BLAMING

A woman at peace has stopped
looking for someone to blame.
—BARBARA JENKINS

One of the key things we need to do in order to own our own lives is to give up blaming anything or anyone for the way our lives are turning out. As long as we blame others, we are putting ourselves in the role of helpless victims, powerless to bring about any change in our circumstances. Yes, bad things have happened to us—people neglected or abandoned us; others disappointed or hurt us; illness and death have affected us and those we love;

jobs are lost; opportunities are missed; people get downsized or outsized—life ain't fair, and we all know it.

But we always have choices. We can live in the problem, blaming life for the bad hand we've been dealt—or we can live in the solution, playing our hand as best we can.

We can give up blaming our parents, our siblings, our bosses, our ancestors, our government, our neighbors, or anyone else for our problems—and instead say, "OK, here's my problem; what am *I* going to do about it?"

- Are you carrying around any resentment or blame for what someone did to you?
- Are you willing to let go of the past and focus on your future instead?
- What would it take for you to forgive and move on?
- What do you have to gain by refraining from blaming?

I think you have to take charge of your own life
and understand that you're either going to live
somebody else's dream or live your own dream.

–WILMA MANKILLER, first woman chief, Cherokee Nation

PREPARE our children for life.

Having a baby gives you a sense of what's really important.

You still work like hell, but it's all in perspective.

—NANCY BADORE, Director, Executive Development Center,
Ford Motor Company

PARENTING 101

"Wait a minute, there's something missing,"
        I thought to myself
        as they pushed me out
        of the hospital
        in a wheelchair,
        clutching my two-day-old infant.
"Where's the instruction manual?
Shouldn't somebody issue
        a handbook of some kind . . .
            an Operator's Guide?"

I was always great at book smarts
        and did well in school.
But I felt lost now
        with no textbook
            on raising a human being.
How would I know what to do?
        They don't teach you this stuff in school.

Parenting is strictly a learn-as-you-go proposition—
    trial and error,
       hit or miss,
         that's how it goes.
On-the-job-training
    with long hours
      and low pay.
Ahh, but the fringe benefits are great—
    that tiny fist clutching your finger,
    that toothless grin of happiness,
    the soft, steady breathing of the tiny person in your arms.
"Looks like it's just you and me, kid,"
    I mutter to my new child.
"We'll just have to figure it out
    as we go along."
Sparkling eyes gaze back at me,
    totally trusting,
      innocent and pure.
"I'll do my best,
    that's all I can promise,"
I reassure us both.
    "And that's all I'll ask of you as well.

WHY?

When my son Michael was six, I took him to a therapist for a year. Michael was an intelligent, sensitive child who excelled in art, music, and English. His problem was his temper. He seemed to get his feelings hurt easily and then overreact by punching some kid's lights out. I had no idea how to help him control his anger or develop thicker skin so other kids wouldn't offend him. Therapy was a great relief for both of us.

Michael saw the therapist (he called him his "temper doctor") every week, and I went with him once a month.

One day I was exasperated—complaining to the shrink, "Why is everything a debate with this kid? Why does he have to argue with me about everything? I'm so exhausted. Why can't he just do what I tell him?"

The temper doctor looked at me and said, "You should be proud of him. . . . You're the one who taught him to think for himself."

I snapped back, "Yes, but he's not supposed to use it on *me!*"

We both burst out laughing as we realized how foolish my retort was.

The shrink was right. And today I'm proud of my son because he's smart, insightful, and nobody's fool. He thinks for himself, and I respect him.

Tips and Tools for Women @ Work

PARENTING WISDOM

Some of the best parenting wisdom I've gotten came from an unexpected source—a guy named Earl whom I dated in the first year after my divorce. Earl never had kids himself, but he some great common sense wisdom about kids ... maybe because he was still a big kid himself! Earl gave me two important tips:

1. Don't sweat the small stuff. If you constantly nag and pick at your kids about every little thing, they'll quickly learn to tune you out. Save your energy for the important things— if you do, then they'll be more likely to listen and heed your words.

2. Kids are like bank accounts. If you invest a lot of time, energy, attention, and love in the early years, it will pay dividends in the later years. You'll have less trouble with them as teens if you have laid a strong foundation of trust and communication in the early years.

These are the two best parenting tips anyone ever gave me.

(continued)

Whom do you turn to for parenting advice? Make a list of the people you think you could ask for wisdom about effective parenting. Then call them up and ask them if they would be willing to share the two or three things they think are most important in being a good parent. Write down their ideas in a little notebook. Collect as many people's comments as you want. Then sort them out and decide which ones make the most sense to you. Try them out. Make a note of what works and what doesn't. Keep the bits of wisdom that work and toss out the rest. Finally, pass them along to your kids when the time comes for them to be parents.

It's not easy being a mother.

If it were easy, fathers would do it.

–DOROTHY (one of TV's *Golden Girls*)

QUESTION **assumptions and old habits.**

Things start as hopes and end as habits.

--LILLIAN HELLMAN, author, playwright, memoirist

WAKING UP

When I was a young wife, I used to iron my husband's shirts every week. He was a snappy dresser and meticulous about his clothes. One weekend he happened to be watching me as I ironed.

"Why do you do it that way?" he asked.

"What?" I replied. "This is just the way it's done."

"Really?" he asked.

"Well, sure," I responded. "You start with the collar and iron that. Then you do the part across the shoulders. Then you iron one sleeve, and the other. Finally, you start on the front side with the buttons and work your way around to the back of the shirt and end on the front side with the button holes. That's the way it's done."

Seemingly amused, he asked, "Who says?"

"Well, that's the way my mother did it," I answered. And it suddenly occurred to me that I ironed shirts the way my mother did without ever thinking about it! It's as if I absorbed things by osmosis without even being conscious of all I was taking in. I wondered how many other things I just did automatically because that's the way it was done in my family.

Scary thought, to discover that you're living by rote—on automatic pilot—like a programmed robot, unthinking, unconscious.

That day was a long time ago, and since then I've become a lot more conscious. It's as if I fell asleep when I was born and it's taken me all these years to become more and more awake.

Today, I'm grateful for the wake-up calls in my life—incidents, comments, and people who jolt me into new states of awareness. For awareness is the first step to change. I choose to live consciously and examine my habits in order to shed those that no longer serve me.

What habits would *you* like to discard?

Nothing in life is more corroding than habit.

–GERTRUDE ATHERTON, historical novelist

Tips and Tools for Women @Work

SOMETIMES THE LITTLE THINGS
CAN MAKE A BIG DIFFERENCE

Are you looking for ways to break old habits—to feel more fulfilled in your life? Don't try to undertake dramatic changes. Instead, focus on lots of little ones.

For instance, look at your bedroom. Ask yourself, "What are three simple things I can do to my bedroom this week that would make me happier?"

1. _____

2. _____

3. _____

Next, focus on your daily work. Ask yourself, "What are three simple things I could do differently in my daily routines this week that would make me happier?"

1. _____

2. _____

3. _____

Ask yourself, "What are three simple things I could do differently in interacting with my spouse (or kids) that would make me happier and improve our relationship?"

1. _____

2. _____

3. _____

You can do this same simple exercise with other aspects of your life: your interactions with friends and family, dealing with neighbors, working with people at your job, and so on. . . .

Assumptions are dangerous things.

–AGATHA CHRISTIE, English mystery writer

REBOUND **from setbacks and failures.**

If you have made mistakes, even serious ones,
there is always another chance for you. What we call
failure is not the falling down, but the staying down.

—MARY PICKFORD, silent screen star

BOUNCING BACK

Life is risky, and even when you think you're doing everything right, sometimes you still fail. You don't get the job you want; a project doesn't turn out right; an agreement gets broken; something you're pursuing disappears; or any of a number of setbacks and disappointments. Being a success at work and in life doesn't mean never making mistakes or never failing. Success has to do with how you *respond* to these setbacks—how well do you bounce back? That's the test of a true winner!

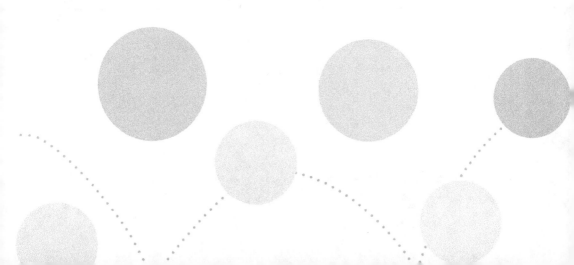

How do you **REBOUND?**

Rethink your strategy.

Explore various options.

Be willing to change direction.

Open your eyes and ears for new opportunities.

Understand that life involves both successes and setbacks.

Never give up on yourself.

Dive into your next adventure.

Tips and Tools for Women @ Work

REBOUNDABILITY

Able to rebound. How do you develop the ability to bounce back from setbacks and disappointments? Is it something you're born with or something you can learn?

The answer is both. Watch a toddler learning to walk. She gets up and starts moving, taking awkward steps on her chubby little legs. Her balance is precarious—then she falls down. Sometimes she cries—often she doesn't. She may give up and crawl for a while. But sooner or later (usually sooner) she gets back up and starts walking again. This is the natural resiliency that you and I were born with—everyone is born with it. We fall down; we get back up. We reach for something and miss; we reach again. Infants and toddlers are superb role models of reboundability.

But reboundability is also something we can develop—our resiliency muscles are already there from childhood, but perhaps we've neglected to keep them strong. Somewhere along the line, some of us gave up and stopped trying when we experienced

setbacks or failures. Perhaps someone told you to "Give up, don't put yourself out there" or "You'll never make it—you're a failure." If people told you things like that, it's hard not to listen to them, especially if they were people you looked up to. But you're an adult now, and those voices don't serve you well.
How can you develop your resiliency muscles?

- Read inspirational stories of people who have overcome incredible obstacles and barriers in their lives. Let their stories inspire you and teach you what you need to learn to overcome in your own life.
- Watch the Special Olympics on TV and see how people with physical and mental challenges have triumphed over their limitations.
- Watch movies like *The Miracle Worker*, or *Million Dollar Baby*, or *Racing Stripes* that tell tales of individuals bouncing back.
- Make a list of all the things you have going for you—talents, skills, abilities, resources, attitudes, contacts, and so on. Keep this list with you (in your appointment book or your wallet or purse). Get it out and read it if you start to get discouraged and want to give up on yourself.

The greatest mistake you can make in life is
to be continually fearing you will make one.

—ELBERT HUBBARD, philosopher, editor, publisher, and author

SEEK spiritual sustenance.

Without faith, nothing is possible.

With faith, nothing is impossible.

—MARY MCLEOD Bethune, civil rights activist

SOUL FOOD

As a spiritual being, it's as important to me to nourish my soul as it is to nourish my body and my mind. Maybe even more so. For if my soul withers, it's difficult, if not impossible, for any other part of me to flourish. I am, after all, a spiritual being having a human experience—not vice versa.

I feed my soul in a variety of ways:

- I stop whatever I'm doing and go outside to watch an especially beautiful sunset. I drink it in with my eyes. I watch it change colors as the sun sinks slowly (sometimes quickly) over the mountains or into the ocean, depending on what time of year it is.
- I bury my face in my dog's soft fur and hold her small body close to mine. Or I gaze into her soulful brown eyes, and connect with her on some deep primitive level. Ah, the Zen of dogs.
- I write with paper and pen as often as I can. Paper has soul—computers don't. I especially relish using textured papers, handmade paper, colored paper, and I touch it and hold it, enjoying the feel on my fingertips.
- I eat soul foods—whole foods. Pomegranates and oranges, berries and peaches—fresh from the tree or bush if I can get them. Vegetables grown in the soil—carrots, potatoes, and

beets—and vegetables grown close to the soil—squash, egg-plant, tomatoes, artichokes, and beans. Earthy food is soul food.

• I surround myself with textures and colors: old quilts, rough-hewn wood, blown glass, collages, assemblages, handmade pottery, silky pillows, fluffy towels, tile countertops, a shiny copper teakettle, fresh flowers, baskets, old denim jeans worn so soft they feel like velveteen, hand-knitted scarves, a vase of peacock feathers—the more variety of textures and colors, the better!

Have you fed your soul today?

Certain thoughts are prayers. There are moments when, whatever be the attitude of the body, the soul is on its knees.

—VICTOR HUGO, French poet, novelist, dramatist

Tips and Tools for Women @ Work

INSPIRING WOMEN

Where do we look for inspiration? Dr. Rachel Naomi Remen writes in her book, *Kitchen Table Wisdom:*

> *When we haven't the time to listen to each other's stories we seek out experts to teach us how to live. The less time we spend together at the kitchen table, the more how-to books appear in the stores and on our bookshelves.... Because we have stopped listening to each other, we may even have forgotten how to listen, stopped learning how to recognize meaning.*

We don't need experts with PhDs to tell us how to live wonderful lives. We need only look to other women. Our world abounds with inspiring women—women who overcome seemingly impossible difficulties, women who follow their dreams into uncharted territory, women who rise to incredible heights of achievement and success. Inspiring women teach us how to find spiritual fulfillment, creative expression, and deep personal satisfaction in life.

Who feeds our souls with spiritual food? Other women do, that's who.

- Make a list of the women who have inspired you. How did they feed your spirit?
- Was your mother a source of inspiration to you? Your aunt? A grandmother? Another female family member?
- Are there women who serve as your spiritual guides and teachers? Who are they? Have you turned to them lately for spiritual sustenance?

The very least you can do in your life is to figure out what you
hope for. And the most you can do is live inside that hope.
Not admire it from a distance but live right in it, under its roof.

—BARBARA KINGSOLVER, novelist

TAKE GOOD CARE **of ourselves.**

You, yourself, as much as anyone in the entire universe,

deserve your love and affection.

—THE BUDDHA

WOMEN WHO GIVE TOO MUCH

"What would radical self-care look like for you?" my friend Beth asks me. It's one of the most important questions anyone has ever asked me. It's the kind of query that, if you take it seriously, can transform your life. It has mine.

Self-care is a challenge for many women. Most of us are socialized as nurturers who take care of others. All too often we put our mates, our kids, our extended families, our bosses, our friends, our neighbors, our community or church commitments first—while putting ourselves last. We are taught to be selfless and self-sacrificing—some of us even achieving status of martyr or saint.

We are women who give too much. We give our time, talent, energy, attention, love, nurturing, caring, money, space, and everything else we have.

But you can't give what you don't have. We must learn to love ourselves first, if we hope to love others fully and well. How can the caretaker take care if she is depleted, exhausted, running on empty? She can't. And worse, she's in danger of becoming resentful, angry, and bitter—toward herself and those she loves.

Charity begins are home. We must love ourselves enough to take care of ourselves *first*.

I like those instructions they give on airplanes before takeoff:

> *In the unlikely event of a sudden change in air pressure in the cabin, oxygen masks will drop from the compartment above your head. Please put on your own mask first before you attempt to help your children or others.*

What would radical self-care look like for *you* today?

Tips and Tools for Women @ Work

WATER RX

There is something restorative about water—the sound of water, the sight of water, the feel of water on our skin. When you need to refresh and/or renew, try some water....

- Drink a tall glass of cool water. Drink it slowly; don't hurry. Feel the way it quenches your thirst, refreshing you from the inside out.
- Splash some warm water (not too warm) on your face. Cup your hands under the faucet and bring your face down to meet the small pond held between your palms. Do it again and again. Repeating, refreshing waves splashing over your countenance—let the water wash away your tension, fears, worries, fatigue.
- Draw a luxurious bath, with or without bubbles. Make the water nice and hot—not so hot as to be painful—but hot enough to relax stiff joints, knotted muscles, fatigued limbs. Gently immerse yourself in your soothing tub, then lean back and rest—let the water do its work. Soak for as long as

you like, adding more hot water as need be. Slip down
in
the tub so your head goes under water too, so your neck
and scalp and face can feel the soothing warmth. When
you're done, pat yourself dry with the biggest, fluffiest
towel you own.

- Seek out a watery place in nature—a creek, a river, an
ocean, a lake, a stream, a waterfall. Feast your senses on the
water—the sight of it, the sounds of it, the fresh moist
smell of it. Absorb the soothing beauty of the water by
watching, listening, breathing in.
- Create a water oasis in your home—a table fountain, an
aquarium, a simple bowl of water with flowers floating in it.
Let your eyes take in the calm of your water oasis.
- Look for creative ways to be around or in water. It will
quench the thirst of your mind and spirit, and body.

The only way you know you love yourself (or anyone else)
is by the commitments you're willing to make and keep.

—DR. PATRICIA ALLEN, therapist, author

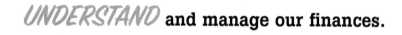 *UNDERSTAND* **and manage our finances.**

Money isn't everything. . .

but it ranks right up there with oxygen.

–RITA DAVENPORT, humorist, speaker, author

A WOMAN AND HER MONEY

Germaine Greer once wrote that a woman must have her own money if she is to be truly her own woman. At the time I read this, I didn't understand it, because I had never really been on my own. I had gone directly from my father's house to my husband's house . . . and then back to my father's house when my marriage broke up. I then returned to college, finishing a BA degree and pursuing a PhD, while living on student loans, scholarships, child support, and financial help from my parents. It wasn't until I was thirty that I left my studies and accepted a full-time job.

I'll never forget how I felt when I got that first real paycheck. There was a rush of pride and self-confidence as I opened the envelope and looked at the check. I suddenly knew what Greer had been writing about. Her words echoed in my mind, and I nodded silently, as if she were right there in my office and could see me acknowledging her wisdom. Thanks, Germaine, you were right about the money. Now I understand.

WHAT TO DO WITH MONEY . . .

Make it.

Own it.

Never waste it.

Enjoy it.

Yak about it.

All prosperity begins in the mind and is dependent only upon the full use of our creative imagination.

–RUTH ROSS, psychologist and author of *Prosperity Principles*

A MAN IS NOT A FINANCIAL PLAN

The seminar speaker was a banker from Salt Lake City giving us the inside scoop on financial planning issues for women. We all cracked up when we heard her say, "A man is not a financial plan."

We knew that secretly, deep down inside, many of us single women still cling to the faint hope that getting a husband will resolve our financial insecurities. None of us would ever admit it publicly, of course, but that fairy-tale myth still lives on in our heart of hearts. You know the myth I'm talking about—the one where the handsome prince comes galloping in on his white horse to carry us away and take care of us forever.

And the married women at the seminar laughed the hardest, because they know for sure that the myth is a lie!

So we listened attentively to the speaker, got out our calculators and pencils and took good notes; we vowed to learn Quicken or QuickBooks as soon as we could free up a weekend.

As for me, I'm a slow learner when it comes to this stuff. . . . I'm still trying to memorize, "A man is not a financial plan."

Tips and Tools for Women @ Work

FOLLOW THE MONEY

Money is tricky stuff. It's powerful, almost mystical. Some people kill for money; many fight for money. There never seems to be enough of it, and yet it's commonly said that money won't buy happiness.

Money is all tied up with control, power, love, self-esteem, identity, ego, and the way people relate to one another. Money can destroy friendships and families.

Money is the last taboo. People will openly discuss their sex lives, their addictions, their foibles and failures, but ask them about their money and watch them clam up.

So what are we to do about this slippery emotional stuff we call money? We must count our money and make our money count. We must resist the temptation to abdicate our fiscal accountability to the men in our lives—whether they're our husbands or our accountants. Above all, we must bring money out of the closet, demystify it, talk about it, shine the light of day on it. For if we don't take control of our money, it will likely control us.

(continued)

What are three simple things you can do today to feel more in charge of your financial well-being?

1. _____

2. _____

3. _____

If you want greater prosperity in your life,

start forming a vacuum to receive it.

—CATHERINE PONDER, prosperity author

VEER AWAY **from negative people.**

Keep away from people who try to belittle your ambitions.
Small people always do that, but the really great
make you feel that you, too, can become great.

–MARK TWAIN, American writer and folksy philosopher

ATTITUDE IS *EVERYTHING!*

Which of these women are you?

Approachable		Angry
Teachable		Testy
Tireless		Tiresome
Inspired	*or*	Irritable
Terrifically optimistic		Terribly pessimistic
Upbeat		Upset
Determined		Depressed
Eager to find solutions		Eager to assign blame

WET BLANKETS

There are plenty of colorful terms for negative people—grumps, grouches, cynics, pessimists, misanthropes, curmudgeons, wet blankets, grumpypants, among others. I used to refer to my then-husband as "El Groucho" because he was always ready to rain on my parade. (Any wonder he's now an ex?)

What can you do about such folks? Well, if you're married to one, you might have to think like a duck and just let his rain of negativity roll off your back. Or follow Paul Simon's advice in "Fifty Ways to Leave Your Lover."

If the grumpypants is not a family member, that makes it easier for you to avoid her or him. Why do you want to avoid this person?

- Negativity is contagious—it's too easy to get caught up in others' whining and complaining.
- Negativity does nothing to solve a problem—it just keeps you mired in despair, frustration, and hopelessness.
- You're judged by the company you keep—if you hang around chronic critics and complainers, others may see you that way, too.

Refuse to let others enroll you in their negative outlook. Remember, happiness is a *choice* . . . and so is unhappiness.

Tips and Tools for Women @ Work

AIKIDO

The martial arts have become quite popular in the past couple of decades. Judo, karate, Tai Kuan Do, and Aikido, among others, have developed an enthusiastic following in the Western world. I like the ideas and philosophy of Aikido in particular, though I never took any training in it—I'm a little nervous about being flipped and falling down on purpose. (I do enough falling down accidentally!) But my son loved his Aikido training, and he taught me some of the philosophy behind the martial art.

Aikido is primarily a defensive martial art—not for offensive attack but for defensive protection. I like that.

If a person is coming at you in attack mode, the natural human inclination is to push back in response—to meet force with force. Aikido teaches a response that is counterintuitive— to step aside as the force is coming upon you, to grab hold of that person's energy, and use his own attack energy to flip and disarm him. Brilliant!

The first thing I need to do is step aside . . . veer out of the path of the oncoming force of the other person. Sometimes that's all I need to do . . . just step out of the way and let him zoom on by. Other times, I may need to step out of the way but also channel his energy to defuse him.

This is usually done on a verbal and emotional level, not physical—since it is rare that someone comes at me in a physical attack mode. But people certainly come at me in verbal or emotional assaults.

If this notion appeals to you, you might want to get a good book on Aikido basics or check out a local Aikido training center (called a *dojo*) in your community. It's a great skill to learn for verbal and emotional self-defense.

Most people are about as happy

as they make up their minds to be.

—ABRAHAM LINCOLN, sixteenth American president

**_WORK_ for peace—in our hearts,
in our homes, in our work.**

We must *be* the change we wish to see in the world.

—MAHATMA GANDHI, who led India to independence
from Britain with his philosophy of nonviolence

PEACEMAKERS

Women want peace.
We settle the squabbles
        between our kids.
We soothe the frustrations
        of our men.
We placate demanding
        bosses.
We mediate between
        warring neighbors.

We are the queens of compromise
        and negotiation.

If women ran the world
        there would be less fighting
                and more talking.
We would work out our conflicts
        with words
                instead of guns.

Road rage would disappear
        and
no one would ever get shot
        on a freeway.

Little League games might be hysterical,
        but never violent.

Women might scream and cry,
        but we would rarely stab or shoot.

And wars would be kept to a minimum,
        because women don't want to send
                their husbands, brothers, and sons to war.

Women give life gladly . . .
        we take life only reluctantly.
We are natural peacemakers,
        homemakers,
                love makers.
It must have been a woman who first said,
        "Make love, not war."

Tips and Tools for Women @ Work

PEACEMAKING BEGINS AT HOME

After the terrorist attacks of September 11, 2001, many people were asking themselves and each other, "How can we stop the terrorism? How can we bring a halt to violence in the world?"

It probably sounds a little 60s-ish, but I always liked that slogan, "Think globally and act locally." If I want to contribute to peace in the world, there are hundreds, if not thousands of things I can do—today, here, now.

- Smile at people I meet on the street.
- When someone cuts in front of me on the freeway, forgive that person cheerfully.
- Let the other guy have the parking spot.
- Seek peaceful resolution to problems with neighbors.
- Clean up the mess someone else's dog made.
- Paint over graffiti.
- Contribute time and resources to the local school.

- Mentor disadvantaged kids.
- Read a book or take a class on conflict resolution.
- Make it a point never to yell in anger at anyone.
- Let go of resentments as fast as they come up.

What are *you* willing to do to make and keep the peace?

Every day we do things, we are doing things that have to do with
peace. If we are aware of our life . . . , our way of looking at things,
we will know how to make peace right in the moment, we are alive.
—THICH NHAT HANH, Vietnamese Buddhist monk and author

Peace is not a relationship of nations. It is a condition of mind

brought about by a serenity of soul. Peace is not merely

the absence of war. It is also a state of mind. Lasting peace

can come only to peaceful people.

—JAWAHARLAL NEHRU, prime minister of India

XPLORE and *XPRESS* our creativity.

There is only one of you in the world, just one.
And if that is not fulfilled, then something has been lost.
—MARTHA GRAHAM, dancer, choreographer

Creativity comes from trust. Trust your instincts.
—RITA MAE BROWN, feminist, writer, educator

COPYCAT

One Christmas, when I was about five, I recall shopping with my mother in a department store that was all decked out for the holidays and stocked with festive decorations for the home. Mom looked admiringly at some interesting Styrofoam Christmas trees. I watched her sizing them up, taking in the details. Suddenly she announced, "I can do that," and then moved on to finish our shopping.

The next thing I remember is Mom in the kitchen with sheets of 2-inch thick Styrofoam, ribbon, small glass ornaments, and bits of artificial holly and berries. She drew patterns on paper first, then used the patterns to cut several different-sized Christmas tree shapes out of the foam. She cut a few holes in the trees and then suspended a glass ornament in each hole. She put a star on top of each tree, stuck the holly and berries on the tips of tree limbs, and glued a few big sequins here and there to finish decking the trees. She cut out a Styrofoam base for each tree, wrapped each in ribbon and affixed them to the trees using pins and glue.

Voilà! A whole forest of trees our very own! I was so impressed and proud of my mom. She was a skillful copycat—a form of creativity that is not widely acknowledged. Mom could dissect something with her eyes, figure out its components and assembly—then go home and recreate it for far less money. She's like a musician who plays by ear—who can hear a composition once, then immediately perform it perfectly.

How many times have you seen something pretty and said to yourself, "I could do that"? The important thing is my mom always followed through. That's what's rare—following through on our creative impulses. Next time you hear yourself say (or think), "I could do that," go *do* it!

Tips and Tools for Women @ Work

Discovering Your Brand of Creativity

Creativity takes many forms. There are people who can invent something from nothing—and others who can take two (or more) things and combine them into something new. There are those who are skillful at solving problems—mechanical, financial, mathematical, scientific, or architectural. Some people excel at bringing people together, while others fly solo with their creativity. What forms does your creativity take?

___	**Mechanical**	___	**Interpersonal**
___	**Musical**	___	**Entrepreneurial**
___	**Visual arts**	___	**Medical**
___	**Cooking**	___	**Scientific**
___	**Community building**	___	**Design**
___	**Gardening**	___	**Decoration**
___	**High tech**	___	**Fashion**
___	**Performing**	___	**Writing**
___	**Spiritual**	___	**Organizing**

Celebrate your own personal creative expressions!

YEARN **and learn for personal growth.**

Energy is the essence of life. Every day you decide how
you're going to use it by knowing what you want and
what it takes to reach that goal, and by maintaining focus.

—OPRAH WINFREY, TV talk show host, actress,
producer, media entrepreneur

What Is a Grownup?

When I was a little girl I looked at grownups as people who had "arrived." They seemed stable, somehow complete in their growth, finished products.

Then I became a grownup and discovered that I had been mistaken. I still kept changing, learning, growing, evolving. I longed to be finished— "done"—but it never happened.

I see now that most people continue to evolve and change throughout their entire lives. We read books; we experience events that alter our perspectives; we continue to strive to understand ourselves and others. We all continue to blossom in new ways, much as a rose unfolds its petals in ever-changing configurations each day.

I would hope that, in the process, we gain some measure of self-awareness and self-acceptance. That's not the same as complacency or resignation. No, it's the peace that comes from appreciating right where you are on the journey of life . . . knowing that the journey is ongoing and that as long as you're living, personal growth will continue. Ain't that great?

People take different roads seeking

fulfillment and happiness. Just because they're not

on *your* road doesn't mean they've gotten lost.

—H. JACKSON BROWN, JR., who wrote *Life's Little Instruction Book*
as a gift for his son who was leaving home for college

It's never too late to become what you might have been.

—GEORGE ELIOT, English female novelist (Mary Ann Evans)
who wrote under a male pseudonym

Tips and Tools for Women @ Work

OPPORTUNITIES FOR PERSONAL GROWTH

We are fortunate to live in a time when there are so many avenues for personal growth and emotional/psychological/spiritual development. A veritable feast for the mind/body/soul is available to almost everyone—books, seminars, therapists, healers, spiritual directors, shamans, gurus, retreats, twelve-step programs, workshops, pilgrimages, meditation centers, yoga teachers, martial arts dojos, churches, synagogues, schools, priests, rabbis, imams, clinics of all types, and much, much more.

- What paths of personal growth attract you?
- How much time, energy, and money are you willing to invest in your personal development?
- Is there some personal pain you want to heal?
- Is there a particular goal you want to achieve?
- What does happiness look like to you?
- What does success look like to you?

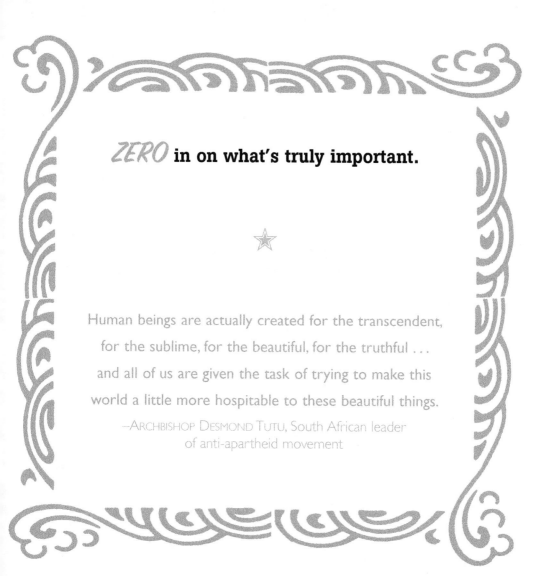

ZERO **in on what's truly important.**

Human beings are actually created for the transcendent,
for the sublime, for the beautiful, for the truthful . . .
and all of us are given the task of trying to make this
world a little more hospitable to these beautiful things.

—ARCHBISHOP DESMOND TUTU, South African leader
of anti-apartheid movement

EPIPHANY

Material girl?

Nope, not me.

I used to long for riches,
daydream about fame and fortune,
fantasize about winning the lottery.

But now I know
I was mistaken.
I discovered that
the best things in life
aren't things.

Hugs and smiles,
laughter and love,
family and friends
now those are *real* treasures.

Tips and Tools for Women @Work

TAKING AIM

How do I know when I'm on target? With so many distractions around me, how can I keep my focus on what's truly important?

Since I'm a visual person (aren't we all?) I use visual images in every way I can. I draw a target . . .

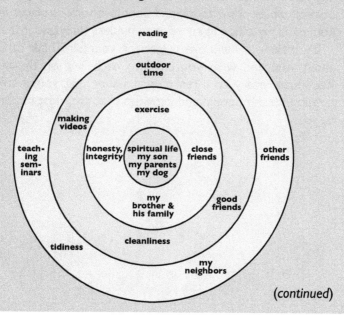

(continued)

And then I write the people, activities, projects, things, goals, and values in the various rings of the target. I think carefully as I do this. I place only the very most important elements in the bull's eye. (Warning: If you put too many things in the bull's eye, you'll be frustrated trying to do justice to them all.) I make several copies of my target and post it in various places in my home and my office to serve as reminders throughout the day.

Try making a bull's-eye target for yourself. Think carefully about who and what you put into each ring on the target. Reevaluate every so often to make sure that you're still on target with the people and activities that are most important to you.

First we receive the light, then we impart it.
Thus we repair the world.

—THE KABBALAH

AND FINALLY . . .

Women are AMAZING . . .

Accomplished

Movers and shakers

Achievers

Zealous

Influential

Networking

Go-getters

ABOUT THE AUTHOR

BJ Gallagher is a storyteller, both by inclination and by profession. Her Irish heritage blessed her with a natural gift of gab, and her stories enrich and enliven her books and seminars. "People forget facts and figures," she says, "but they remember good stories." BJ uses stories to teach important lessons about how to live a good life, create authentic friendships, and do fulfilling work.

Her own women's work runs the gamut from cocktail waitress to corporate middle manager, including stints as intern in a congressman's office, secretary for a studio of graphic artists, sales trainer for car dealerships, ghost writer for a CEO, career counselor, and university adjunct professor. She has been a stay-at-home wife as well as a single working mother with a latchkey kid. She is a Phi Beta Kappa graduate of the University of Southern California, and earned her advanced degree from the School of Hard Knocks. Her crazy-quilt working life makes her an expert on the vast range of activities that can rightly be called women's work.

BJ has written ten books, including the international best-seller, *A Peacock in the Land of Penguins* (Berrett-Koehler; 2001). Her most recent books include *Everything I Need to Know I Learned from Other Women* (Conari; 2002) and *Friends Are Everything* (Conari; 2005).

You can contact BJ at *www.bjgallagher.com*.

Printed in the USA
CPSIA information can be obtained
at www.ICGtesting.com
JSHW052018140824
68134JS00027B/2531

9 781684 421176